Netball

Table of Contents

Written by Kassi Gilmour

Team sports are enjoyed by many people, but did you know that netball is the most popular team sport played by girls? It is also the fourth most popular team sport for children.

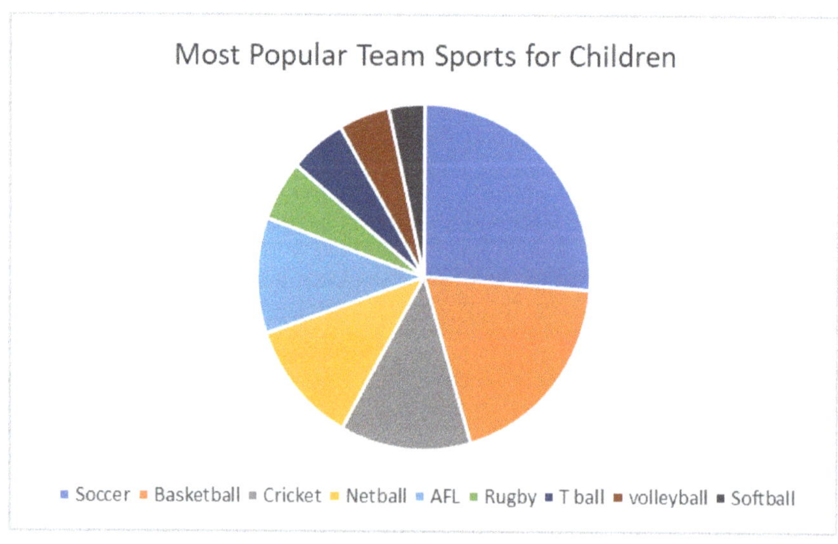

data from roymorgan.com, July 2023

Netball is a fast ball game
played on flat ground. Two
teams play against each other,
and the team with the most
goals wins.

Over time, netball has grown
and developed into the game we
know today.

Netball was known as girls' basketball and evolved over time. In the beginning, a female sports teacher asked for a copy of the *basketball* rules.

The rules included a *diagram* with arrows to show where players may want to *patrol*. The

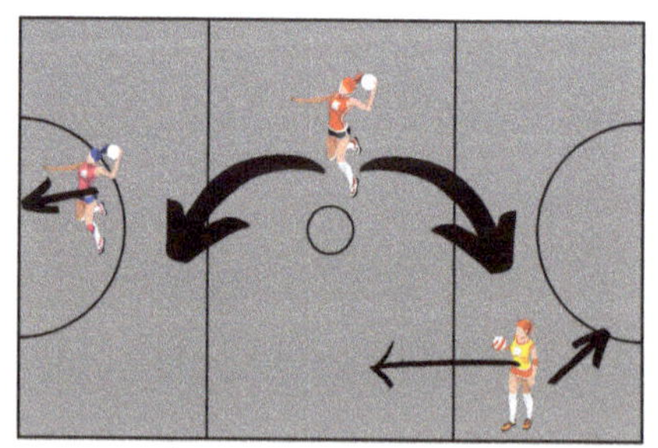

sports teacher saw this as rules for where players could and couldn't go.

Because girls found it difficult to run and dribble a ball with long skirts, dribbling and running with the ball were eliminated from the game.

RULES

A netball ground is shaped like a rectangle. It is divided into three parts.

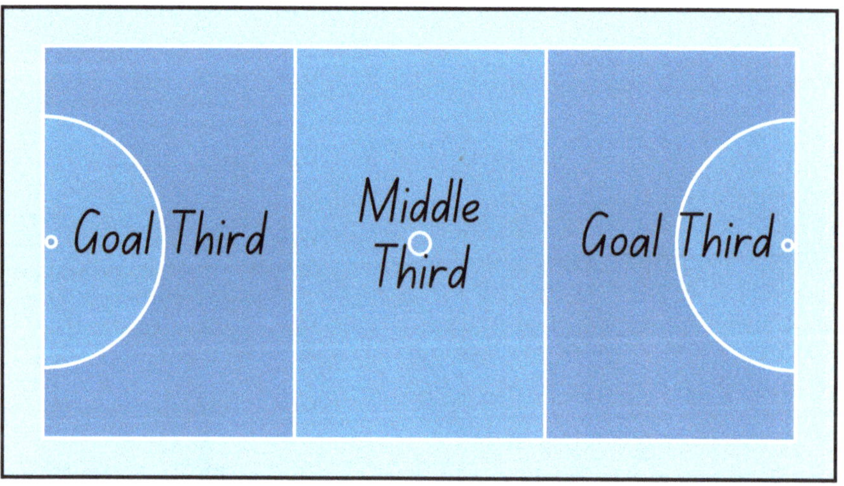

There are two goal-thirds and one middle-third.

In each of the goal thirds, there is an arc painted on the ground. Goal shooting must occur within the arc. A tall post with a hoop sits at both ends.

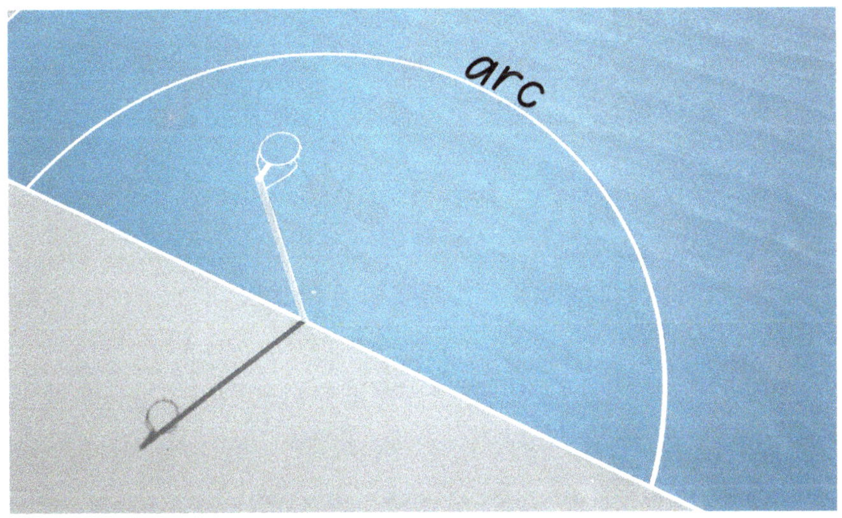

Each team may have 7 players, and they are all given a different role and spot to play within.

These roles are:
- Goal Shooter (GS)
- Goal Keeper (GK)
- Wing Defender (WD)
- Wing Attack (WA)
- Goal Defender (GD)
- Goal Attack (GA), and
- Middle (C)

Each player must stay in their allocated spots.

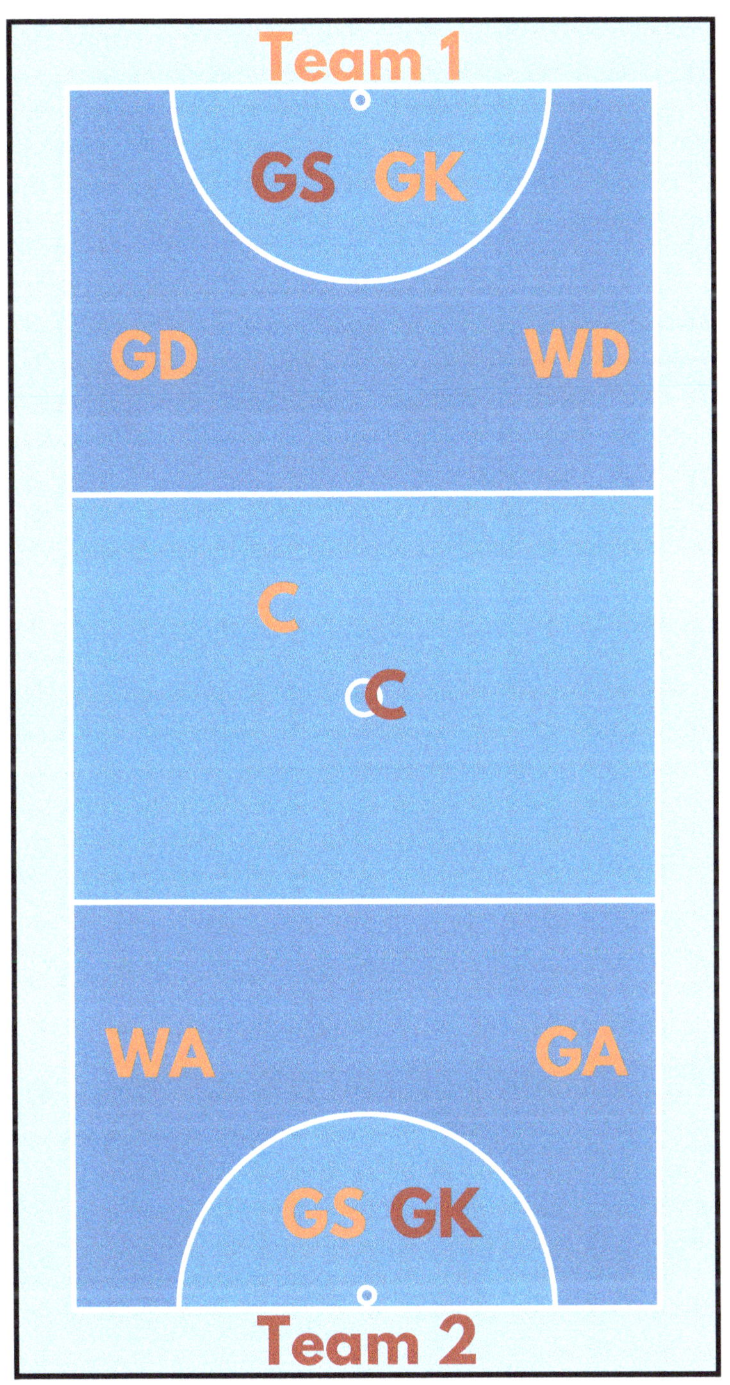

Team 1
GS GK
GD WD
C
C
WA GA
GS GK
Team 2

A netball game lasts for 60 minutes and is split into four equal times.

A goal is recorded when a player in the goal third throws the ball into the hoop.

Players cannot run with the ball because taking a step after getting the ball will result in the team losing control of it.

When a player gets the ball, they must throw it within three seconds.

You must keep your feet three *feet* away from any player who has the ball.

If you drop the ball and pick it up again, the other team gets the ball.

The ball cannot be thrown over one-third of the playing zone.

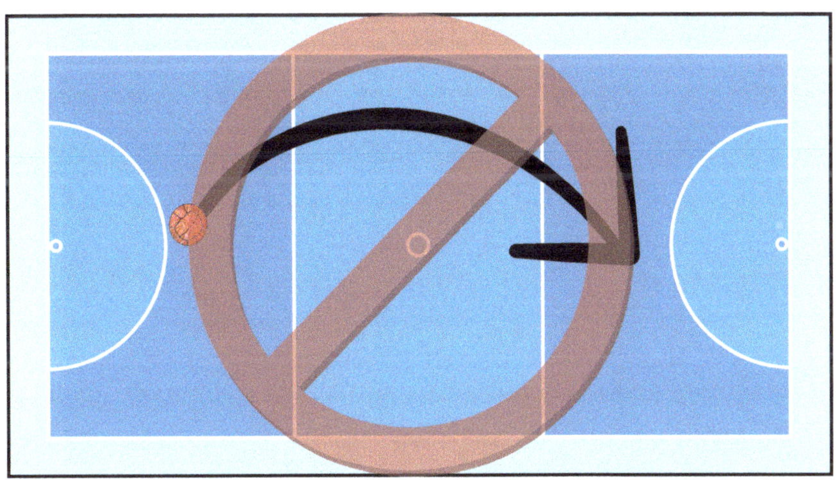

If the ball leaves the playing zone, the team that threw it out must give it to the other team.

UNIFORMS

Netball can be played in any clothes, and a bib is worn over a shirt. The bib shows which team a player is on and what part they play.

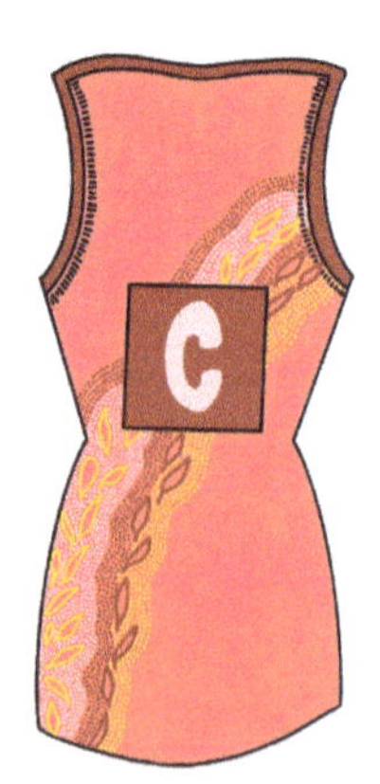

Some competitive netball teams have dresses.

TEAMS

There are many netball teams. Most are local to where people live, but amazing players are selected to play for a job.

They train really hard and travel all over the *globe* to compete.

GLOSSARY

This page is not decodable and may be read to the child.

arc - semi-circle.

bib - a cloth worn over the chest.

basketball - a team sport ball game.

competitive - organised teams that play to win.

diagram - a hand-drawn image.

dribble - bouncing the ball while moving forward.

feet - a measurement of length, 30cm.

globe - the earth.

goal - ball passes through the net to score a point.

ground - court.

middle - centre.

patrol - guarding and moving in an area.

shooting - throwing the ball.

spot - position.

team - a group of players on one side.

zone - court.

INDEX

Questions:

1. How did netball begin?
2. What are some of the rules?
3. Describe a netball court.
4. Why do players need to wear a bib?
5. What sport have you played? What is the same or different about your sport?

Vowels

The graphemes 'ur' and 'ir' represent the r-controlled vowel phoneme /er/, as in turn and girl.

The graphemes 'u_e' and 'ew' represent the long vowel phoneme /o͞o/, as in flute and drew.

These pictures help you remember the sound.